TRUMPERICKS

TRUMPERICKS

A Doggerel Journey Through the Twisted Mind of Donald Trump

ROBERT M. STONE

Illustrated by Chris Critelli

ISBN-13: 9781978255043
ISBN-10: 1978255047

For my loving and very patient wife Nancy, who asked solicitously whenever she saw my blank stare, "Are you thinking of another limerick?"

R.M.S.

For my parents, who always made sure there were enough pencils and paper in the house. And for my friends, who graciously put up with me drawing them all the time.

C.B.C.

Dear Alice,
Hope This brings you a smile!

- Chris Critelli

AUTHOR'S PREFACE

This did not begin as an effort to write a book. Instead, the first of what would become "Trumpericks" were written as a visceral reaction to the firing of James Comey. After that, on an almost daily basis, I was moved by events to write more verses. My "creative process" consisted of watching morning news shows (especially MSNBC's *Morning Joe*), reading the newspaper, becoming upset, and sitting at the computer keyboard to compose. I began posting individual limericks on social media and developed somewhat of following. As the volume of verses grew, friends and family encouraged me to publish them. I owe those friends and family members a debt of gratitude for their support and encouragement.

I also want to thank my talented and clever illustrator, Chris Critelli, for joining this project and enhancing the book with his artwork. Finding him was serendipitous. The result was stupendous.

NOTE FROM THE ILLUSTRATOR

Thanks, Bob! Thanks for coming along with the perfect pairing of word and wit! Like a sumptuous wine to go along with the stinky cheese of my cartoon chronicling.

Every cartoonist has to find an angle with their subject. A point of view. A focus. And when that subject is Donald Trump, an interesting challenge presents itself; how to caricature a man who is, himself, a living caricature? For me, I decided early on *not* to try and capture my "perfect version" of Trump in this book. Instead, my goal was to make every image of him distinct. In every illustration, hopefully, we're seeing a different side of Donald Trump. The braggart. The child. The con man. The fool. The fox. The existential threat.

I focused on his shiftiness, his innate elasticity. Whether morally, financially, ethically, legally, with matters of truth or objective reality -- Trump is bendy. He's a shape-shifter. Almost like some bombastic genie who'll morph and contort himself into anything, promising to make our wildest dreams come true. But as with most genies (and all grifters), the wish-granting usually comes at too high a price. And those wild dreams turn to ether.

Anyway, please have fun with our book!

INAUGURATION DAY
(OR SIZE MATTERS)[1]
JANUARY 20, 2017

Nearly everyone in our great nation
was attending my inauguration.
It was boisterous and loud
and a world-record crowd,
millions showing their appreciation.

They were stretched from the National Mall
past Chicago and out to St. Paul.
So imagine my shock,
when (compared to Barack)
the true size of my turnout was small.

MUSLIM, UH ER...TRAVEL BAN
JANUARY 27, 2017

I campaigned for a full Muslim ban.
How I wish we could stick to that plan.
But it smacks (just a smidgeon)
of rule based on religion,
like the stuff they would do in Iran.

So we'll call it restriction on travel
(till some flaky judge brings down the gavel).
Say it's countries, not sect.
Will this label protect
a slick scheme that is bound to unravel?

To keep out each berserk terrorist,
seven nations are on the blacklist.[2]
I'll invoke 9/11,
though they weren't from these seven.[3]
Spare my business partners, I insist.[4]

DEVOS[5]
FEBRUARY 7, 2017

I've great love for the uneducated.
That's why Betsy has been nominated.
She'll transform public schools
into havens for fools
so more Trump devotees are created.

MAR-A-LAGO WHITE HOUSE GOLD MEMBERSHIP[6]
FEBRUARY 11, 2017

An exorbitant membership fee
gets you dinner with Shinzo and me.
And a wonderful perk—
watch diplomacy work,
as we talk global security.

You don't need any government clearance.
Just reserve your choice mealtime appearance.
Take in classified chat.
Hear this tidbit or that.
Secret Service won't run interference.

FLYNN-FLAM MAN
FEBRUARY 13, 2017

I regret to announce that Mike Flynn
is already a Trump-team has-been.
It has great consequence
when you lie to Mike Pence.
At least this will be our preferred spin.[7]

With the Russians he liked to consort.
Sally warned they might try to extort.
But he helped my campaign,
treated Hil with disdain.
So these facts were of zero import.[8]

At my rallies he yelled, "Lock her up!"
Followed me like a motherless pup.
Now the seeds have been sown,
and he's out on his own.
Pretty soon he'll be passing a cup.

WHAT FIRST AMENDMENT?
FEBRUARY 17, 2017

Mainstream news is our worst enemy.
I should ban them if they won't agree.
They report what I do,
and that makes me turn blue.
Joseph Stalin has nothing on me.

Fox and Breitbart are good for our nation.
They give me well-deserved adulation.
And I'd like to see clones
of that sage Alex Jones,[9]
plus a nifty state-run TV station.

 **Donald J. Trump** ✔
@realDonaldTrump

The FAKE NEWS media (failing @nytimes,
@NBCNews, @ABC, @CBS, @CNN) is not my
enemy, it is the enemy of the American People!

2:48 PM - Feb 17, 2017

Donald J. Trump ✓
@realDonaldTrump

Terrible! Just found out that Obama had my "wires tapped" in Trump Tower just before the victory. Nothing found. This is McCarthyism!

4:35 AM - Mar 4, 2017

Donald J. Trump ✓
@realDonaldTrump

Is it legal for a sitting President to be "wire tapping" a race for president prior to an election? Turned down by court earlier. A NEW LOW!

4:49 AM - Mar 4, 2017

OBAMA BUG
MARCH 4, 2017

I'm awake at an ungodly hour,
'cause Barack put a "tapp" in my tower.
He's a very sick guy!
Likely Kenya-born spy!
Tried to stop me from coming to power![10]

Donald J. Trump ✓
@realDonaldTrump

I'd bet a good lawyer could make a great case out of the fact that President Obama was tapping my phones in October, just prior to Election!

4:52 AM - Mar 4, 2017

Donald J. Trump ✓
@realDonaldTrump   ✓ Follow

How low has President Obama gone to tapp my phones during the very sacred election process. This is Nixon/Watergate. Bad (or sick) guy!

5:02 AM - Mar 4, 2017

COURTLY MANNERS[11]
MARCH 17, 2017

Merkel asked, "May I please shake your hand?"
I don't like her so that would seem canned.
Showing typical grace,
I just stared into space,
and now I'm a scoundrel in Deutschland.

DISMANTLING THE ADMINISTRATIVE STATE
(BECAUSE BANNON SAID SO)
MARCH 28, 2017

I love signing executive orders—
flash my signature for the camcorders.
I display these with pride
but don't know what's inside.
It's enough that I please my supporters.

I'm attempting to quickly unwind
prior decrees that were thoughtful and kind.
They were signed by B.O.,
so they'll all have to go.
Those who think he's a Muslim won't mind.[12]

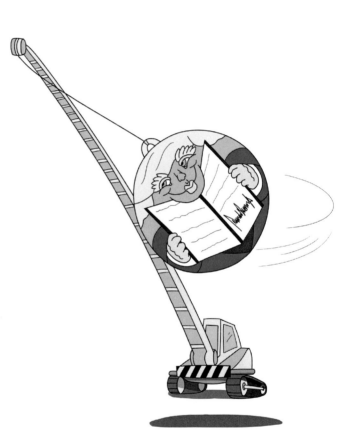

MISSILES OVER SYRIA
APRIL 8, 2017

I denounced this approach in the past,
but I'd love to see Tomahawks blast.
Fifty-nine sent through space
to destroy their airbase.
It's too bad the effect didn't last.[13]

Donald J. Trump ✔
@realDonaldTrump

President Obama, do not attack Syria.
There is no upside and tremendous
downside. Save your "powder" for another
(and more important) day!

6:21 AM - Sep 7, 2013

SPICEY!
APRIL 11, 2017

I just wish news reporters were nicer
to the grim and befuddled Sean Spicer.
He should never defer
to that bitch, Katy Tur.[14]
In his shoes I would slice her and dice her.[15]

Now it really is somewhat bizarre
that Sean likes Adolf more than Bashar.[16]
He should hide in a bush[17]
or get whacked on the tush
or be banished to somewhere afar.

Spicey isn't completely to blame.
Fronting me is a zero-sum game.
He's the butt of mean gags
from those SNL hags.[18]
Credibility he won't reclaim.

TRUMP'S LAMENT
(OR MUSINGS OF A DELUSIONAL MIND)
MAY 12, 2017

I declared, "Here's the deal, Mr. Comey:
it's unquestioning fealty you owe me.
I'm incredibly pissed
that these probes still exist.
You'll be fired if you can't be my homey."[19]

If there's one thing that makes my blood boil,
it's when minions aren't totally loyal.
And I truly despise
the press outing my lies.
They should promptly be banned from our soil. (That I can tell you. Believe me.)

Please address me as "Emperor Trump."
I invented the phrase "prime the pump."[20]
In my new government,
there can be no dissent.
Ask "how high" when I tell you to jump.

I proclaimed to myself, "All is fine,"
after leaning on Rod Rosenstein,[21]
but was sad to discover
that this gave me no cover,
as the press wouldn't fall into line.

My detractors keep pushing to learn
what appears in each Trump tax return.
Not one soul will believe me.
Even Russians deceive me![22]
And the Dems hope I'll just crash and burn.

The press wants everyone to believe
that I'm ignorant, dense, and naïve.
But my riches will grow
as emoluments flow.[23]
It's more stupid to give than receive.

Despite all of those pesky reporters,
I have so many ardent supporters.
If facts disprove their views,
they just call it "fake news."
I want these people guarding our borders.

SHARING[24]
MAY 15, 2017

I told Lavrov, "Our intel's the best.
I've some tidbits to get off my chest.
Since our press isn't here,
I'll share secrets most dear.
Then you tell me where I should invest."

I told Kislyak, "Our intel's so great.
Some examples I'd like to relate.
You have no need to spy.
I'll just declassify.
I'm so happy to reciprocate."

I resent this impeachment discussion.
They behave like I have a concussion.
Accusations unfair!
I'm just anxious to share—
and especially if you are Russian.

NONDENIAL DENIAL
(OR DESTROYING THE CREDIBILITY OF ALL MY ASSOCIATES)
MAY 16, 2017

No one knew that this job would be tough.
Of my critics I've had quite enough!
I lack credible staff
to defend this new gaffe,
so I'll send out H. R. Pufnstuf.[25]

APRES ROD, LE DELUGE?
MAY 17, 2017

By announcing a step that seems huge,
Rosenstein says he won't be my stooge.[26]
With the probe now on track,
will this latest setback
send me in quick descent like a luge?

NATO
(OR MOVE OVER MONTENEGRO OR DONNIE TAKES A FIELD TRIP TO EUROPE)[27]
MAY 26, 2017

It's so sad I was forced to retreat
from my claim that NATO's obsolete.
I suppose if you're rootin'
against my comrade Putin,
our withdrawal would be indiscreet.

In old Brussels I showed them my best—
shoved an ally and puffed out my chest.
NATO friends I berated:
If their debts aren't abated,
our commitments will be reassessed.

Never mind if it's mutual aid.
We won't play without 2 percent paid.
Though to help us they ran
into Afghanistan,
I don't count their lives lost in this trade.

I've concluded that Germany's bad.
They sell cars in our country—so sad![28]
And I'm taking a stance
against Macron of France.
His firm handshake has me hopping mad!
(He's so young that I could be his dad.)
(I prefer to support Leningrad.)
(I consider the EU a fad.)

DAMN JUDGES[29]
MAY 26, 2017

As your emperor I am appalled
with the Fourth Circuit judges (so-called).
If they won't rubber-stamp,
let's send them to a camp.
Just like Mexicans, they should be walled.

BUDGET WOES[30]
MAY 28, 2017

My new budget's incurring much wrath.
What's so wrong with alternative math?
And forgoing your health
for the Trump family's wealth
is the only legitimate path.

EVERY TIME I SPEAK OR TWEET, ANOTHER ENGLISH TEACHER DIES
MAY 28, 2017

"The fake news fabricates made-up lies."
Does this signal good grammar's demise?
Do not fret, all you nerds,
'cause I have the best words.
(Speaking triple redundancy-wise.)

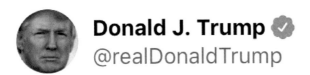

Donald J. Trump ✔
@realDonaldTrump

It is my opinion that many of the leaks coming out of the White House are fabricated lies made up by the #FakeNews media.

5:33 AM · May 28, 2017

COVFEFE
MAY 31, 2017

The fake news outlets always conspire
to paint me as an ignorant liar.
Despite all that covfefe,
Trump fans still love their hefe.
It's blind loyalty I so admire.

 Donald J. Trump ✔
@realDonaldTrump

&+ Follow ⌄

Despite the constant negative press covfefe

RETWEETS   LIKES
98,007   123,306

5:06 AM - 31 May 2017

CLIMATE SCHMIMATE
JUNE 1, 2017

I've withdrawn from the climate accord.[31]
All this science stuff leaves me so bored.
Polar ice melts are fated.
Oxygen's overrated.
Higher profits will be our reward.

You snowflakes think I don't have a soul,
when my mission is just to save coal.
So we'll never have Paris,
and I aim to embarrass
as I forfeit our leadership role.

All the pundits will say that I blew it
by accepting advice from Scott Pruitt.
But those "experts" are jokes:
climate change is a hoax
from the Chinese—and only I knew it.

We'll be drilling and fracking more wells.
No big deal if the carbon count swells.
There's no need to turn blue:
We'll have extra O_2
at my fabulous string of hotels.

I enjoy the sweet smell of methane.
It envelops and tickles my brain.
All these climate change rules
were invented by fools.
Why not flush toxic waste down the drain?

Why do losers continue to seethe?
Is it bad if our children can't breathe?
They should embrace the task,
proudly don a gas mask.
It's this legacy that I bequeath.

Last night tweeting, I had so much fun—
criticized the way London is run.
I expected applause,
but it seems I'm the cause
of alliances coming undone.

Cuba's record on rights I abhor.
We should never have opened that door.[32]
But the Saudis have dough;
Kremlin's running my show.
So their misdeeds I choose to ignore.

 **Donald J. Trump** ✔
@realDonaldTrump

 🐦 Follow

At least 7 dead and 48 wounded in terror attack and Mayor of London says there is "no reason to be alarmed!"

4:31 AM - Jun 4, 2017

COMEY, YOU WERE BELOW ME[33]
JUNE 8, 2017

Comey's memos have caused a sensation.
I wish Congress would take a vacation.
Is it such a great sin
that I tried to save Flynn
and inhibit the investigation?

I have told the Director, "Hey, James,
you don't need to play supercop games.
Michael's such a nice guy.
Won't you let him slip by?
Then he never will have to name names."

AN IMAGINED (AND HIGHLY UNLIKELY) MOMENT OF TRUMP SELF-REALIZATION
JUNE 8, 2017

Contradictions I articulate
make it tough to keep all my lies straight.
It won't be hard to prove:
If you see my lips move,
you will know that I prevaricate.

COMEY, DON'T TRY TO SLOW ME
JUNE 9, 2017

Intel hearings are making me tired.
Guessing my intent isn't required.
Jimmy Comey's no dope—
when the boss says, "I hope…"
it means, "Do what I say or you're fired."[34]

It seems Comey was seeking my doom.
The guy feared being in the same room.
He was far too straight-laced
and integrity based.
So I needed to lower the boom.

UNDER OATH (100 PERCENT)[35]
JUNE 10, 2017

I told Kasowitz, "Don't be forlorn
that I offered to testify sworn.
I'm your most famous client,
and I'm always defiant.
Now my perjury's yours to suborn."

REALITY TELEVISION[36]
JUNE 10, 2017

Anxious newspeople want me to blow
the punch line to this great TV show.
Are recordings with tapes
hiding in White House drapes?
Tune in next week, and maybe you'll know.

TWITTERING MY TIME AWAY
JUNE 12, 2017

As the sixth month in high office nears,
my campaign vows fall far in arrears.
Now my time is best spent
spewing bull excrement,
since I'm so full it's clogging my ears.

DESPOTIC INTENTIONS
JUNE 12, 2017

I've decided it's time to be crueler:
emulate a tyrannical ruler,
have some meek sycophants
kiss the seat of my pants,[37]
float the idea to terminate Mueller.[38]

I might also take out some aggressions
and intimidate little Jeff Sessions—
helping him realize
before he testifies,
it's no good to reveal my transgressions.[39]

I expect loyalty absolute.
Violate this, and you'll get the boot.
Jimmy, Sally, and Preet[40]
sealed their fates as dead meat
when they thought they could play it too cute.

TRAVEL BANS, HOSTAGES, AND STONEWALLING
JUNE 13, 2017

Now the Justice Department is bitter
that the Ninth Circuit quoted my Twitter.[41]
They politely explain:
if I won't self-restrain,
they will send me a strict babysitter.

I was trying to think of someone
to negotiate with Kim Jong-Un.
How about my pal Dennis,
who was on *The Apprentice*?
He's a smooth-talking son of a gun.[42]

Old Jeff Sessions was very alert—
used the privilege I'd failed to assert.
He refused to respond,
thus preserving our bond
and ensuring I wouldn't get hurt.[43]
(and conspiracy remains covert.)

When they tried to pin Jeff to the wall,
he would obfuscate, fabricate, stall.
Never made an admission
or showed any contrition.
Used the mantra, "I cannot recall."

SENATORIAL SEXISM
JUNE 17, 2017

Sessions tried to do me a great service,
but that Kamala made him too nervous.
My men couldn't abide
the fierce skill she applied.
From these tough female lawyers preserve us![44]

MY SPOKESPERSONS
JUNE 19, 2017

Every night before going to bed,
self-destructive tweets flow from my head.
But keep watching your tube,
'cause I'll send out some rube
to deny that I said what I said.

NOT TERROR IF DIRECTED AT MUSLIMS
JUNE 19, 2017

In an act of anti-Islam heat,
fourteen worshippers struck on the street.
But I'm not too concerned
when the tables are turned—
Muslim victims don't merit a tweet.[45]

BLOODY WOMEN
JUNE 29, 2017

All the losers have taken to pleading
that my rants not describe women bleeding.
Whether Mika or Megyn,[46]
there's no point in their beggin',
since misogyny's part of my breeding.

Donald J. Trump
@realDonaldTrump

I heard poorly rated @Morning_Joe speaks badly
of me (don't watch anymore). Then how come
low I.Q. Crazy Mika, along with Psycho Joe,
came..

5:52 AM - Jun 29, 2017

Donald J. Trump
@realDonaldTrump

...to Mar-a-Lago 3 nights in a row around New
Year's Eve, and insisted on joining me. She was
bleeding badly from a face-lift. I said no!

5:58 AM - Jun 29, 2017

REVERSE ROBIN HOOD
JUNE 29, 2017

Poor and elderly voters got played:
they believed I'd preserve Medicaid.
But such help for them ends
with tax breaks for rich friends.
Seems to me an appropriate trade.[47]

KINDRED SPIRITS
(OR CHRIS CHRISTIE GOES TO THE SHORE)
JULY 3, 2017

On a budget we couldn't agree,
so the people are banned from the sea.
My address is dot gov;
privilege fits like a glove.
These restrictions aren't binding on me.[48]

RUSSIA HOUSE
JULY 10, 2017

I told G-20 our nation's cursed
with intelligence that is the worst.[49]
And I aced this big test,
proving I'm at my best
when my comments are made unrehearsed.

Perhaps sensing I'm not very bright,
Putin offered to join in our fight:
so we're cyber secure,
he will help guard our door.
Then we all can sleep better at night.

Wait! They're saying this idea's insane.
Not just Dems but Graham, Sasse, and McCain.
But I never retreat.
I'll just recast my tweet.
Changing narrative isn't a strain.

Little Don is a chip off the block.
It's a talent nobody should mock.
When he gets in a bind,
blithely changes his mind.
Keeps you guessing which version's a crock.[50]

Donald J. Trump @realDonaldTrump

Putin & I discussed forming an impenetrable Cyber Security unit so that election hacking, & many other negative things, will be guarded..
4:50 AM - Jul 9, 2017

Donald J. Trump @realDonaldTrump

The fact that President Putin and I discussed a Cyber Security unit doesn't mean I think it can happen. It can't-but a ceasefire can,& did!
5:45 PM - Jul 9, 2017

THE FRENCH PRESIDENT'S WOMAN
JULY 14, 2017

While in Paris I chatted off-script,
telling Brigitte Macron she looks ripped.[51]
The effluent flows south
from my brain to my mouth.
I'm unable to keep my trap zipped.

MADE-IN-AMERICA WEEK[52]
JULY 18, 2017

It's U.S. manufacture we seek,
for without it our future looks bleak.
Let's have outsourcing banned
(all except the Trump brand,
since what Ivanka sells is unique).[53]

NO MORE REPEAL AND REPLACE[54]
JULY 18, 2017

I announced we'd have health care so great,
but I guess we'll all just have to wait.
Can't repeal and replace.
Now there's egg on my face.
My balloon has begun to deflate.

On the White House lawn, we made a scene:
praised a House bill I later called "mean."
They expect me to lead,
but it's too much to read,
and I much prefer my putting green.

Of the party brass I'm not a fan.
They had seven years to forge a plan.
I thought it would be easy,
but the process is cheesy.
Can we blame this defeat on Iran?

MORE IMAGINED TRUMP SELF-REALIZATION AFTER HIS UNINTELLIGIBLE *NEW YORK TIMES* INTERVIEW[55]
JULY 20, 2017

I think governing's uncomplicated,
'cause I'm willfully uneducated
and unwilling to read
or let facts intercede,
metaphorically decapitated.

I spew incomprehensible gas.
It's so hard to pick through the morass.
Give no apology,
but need proctology
to help extract my head from my ass.

IT'S MUELLER TIME[56]
JULY 21, 2017

Mueller's probing my financial dealing
to determine what I've been concealing:
wants to follow the dough,
see what tax returns show.
This gives me an uncomfortable feeling.

Did the Russians seek some tit for tats,
washing rubles through my laundromats?
Did my special friend Vlad
know that I could be had
if he helped me defeat Democrats?

Asked my lawyers what it would entail
to ensure that this inquest will fail.
Would the pardon route work?
Could I fire the jerk?
Will my shady deals land me in jail?

BOY SCOUT JAMBOREE
JULY 24, 2017

I'm a boorish, imperious lout—
the antithesis of a good Scout.
Am I far too uncouth
to inspire our youth?
This fiasco removes any doubt.[57]

"SKINNY REPEAL," WAR HEROES, AND OTHERS
JULY 28, 2017

I told Mitch I need something to sign.
I don't care if it's mean or benign,
or it's thick or it's thin.
You must give me a win.
Get the lackeys to fall into line.

I insulted a hero of war,[58]
and he's finally evened the score:
joined with Lisa and Susan,
to make sure I keep losin'.
My failed legacy now seems secure.[59]

My deal-making skills hardly amaze.
Bashing senators no longer pays.
No agenda in place,
so I'll shore up my base
by attacking transgenders and gays.[60]

I've made public-relations upgrades:
look to Mooch for some vulgar tirades.[61]
In my clown-car domain,
the swamp never will drain.
I'm creating my own Everglades.

Jeff won't act as my private law firm,
so I'll leave him to dangle and squirm.
Someone this damned disloyal
should be lanced like a boil,
but a successor they won't confirm.[62]

Now I'm getting a new chief of staff,
which should give my detractors a laugh.[63]
Hard at work cleaning house—
no one's safe but my spouse.
Separating the chaff from the chaff.

PEGGY NOONAN HURT MY FEELINGS[64]
JULY 28, 2017

She has called me a weak "drama queen,"
which I think is especially mean.
So you won't see me spoonin'
with that old Peggy Noonan.
Now, excuse me; I have to go preen.

ADVICE FOR MINI-ME
JULY 30, 2017

Scaramucci, I think you're so great.
Just like me but with less height and weight.
So your wife's left your pad.
Don't be worried or sad.
Steve can teach you how to self-fellate.[65]

SO LONG, MINI-ME
(WE HARDLY KNEW YE)[66]
JULY 31, 2017

Kelly told me to ditch little Tony,
since he's crude, brash, and full of baloney.
And some claim that the Mooch
is on coke, weed, or hooch.
Prototype for a president's crony.

DESCENT INTO THE ABYSS
AUGUST 2, 2017

This is feeling like more déjà vu:
leaks forced me to admit what is true.
But there's good reason why
I told Junior to lie.
It's what any nice father would do.[67]

My approval's in rapid descent—
reaching down to touch 30 percent.
But it's never my fault.
Unrelenting assault
has been fueling all this discontent.

My base desperately needs celebration,
so I've asked Congress for legislation.
Join the xenophobe shout:
"Huddled masses, keep out!
Immigrants are destroying our nation."[68]

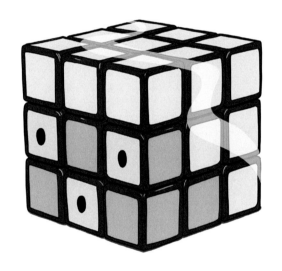

To make our foreign policy great,
I'll just gut the Department of State.
Then I'll isolate Rex,
and our allies I'll vex,
letting Jared determine their fate.[69]

And Ivanka will work "alongside"
General Kelly as he strokes my pride.
He must realize this is
the Trump family biz
and my kin won't have access denied.[70]

Putin keeps proving that he's a thug,
which makes me want to give him a hug.
Congress applied the brakes:
won't let me sleep with snakes
or sweep Russia's wrongs under the rug.[71]

TRUTH OR CONSEQUENCES
(OR FABRICATED PHONE CALLS WITH MEXICAN AND BOY SCOUT LEADERS)[72]
AUGUST 3, 2017

My relation with truth is quite lax.
I believe in alternative facts.
If it seems good to say,
I will send it your way.
When it forms in my head, my mouth quacks.
(Doesn't matter if it's full of cracks.)
(I'm promoting myself to the max.)

WHITE HOUSE DUMP[73]
AUGUST 3, 2017

I'm not meaning to sound like a grump,
but the White House is really a dump.
The decor is nightmarish,
not sufficiently garish.
It is clearly no place for a Trump.

STILL MORE IMAGINED TRUMP SELF-REALIZATION
AUGUST 7, 2017

I'm a serial prevaricator,
not to mention a great bloviator.
Conceit fully displayed—
I believe I'm self-made,
so I only worship my "creator."

Is dissembling a slick form of art
or a ceaseless obnoxious brain fart?
Do I even realize
that I'm telling big lies?
No, I'm light years too far from that smart.

On the other hand, some folks don't care
if my act's a delusion and snare.
They might finally learn,
when the worm starts to turn,
what it meant to hear "buyer beware."

MENTAL DIARRHEA CONCERNING NORTH KOREA
(OR "IF WE HAVE NUCLEAR, WHY CAN'T WE USE IT?")
AUGUST 9, 2017

It's my nature to be bellicose.
Think I'll give North Korea a dose:
threaten fury and fire,
causing Kim to perspire.[74]
Should we kiss our Guam base adios?[75]

In diplomacy I'm a late bloomer—
criticized by McCain and Chuck Schumer.
I was just having fun
with that guy Kim Jong-Un.
But he clearly has no sense of humor.

People say I'm exceedingly reckless,
temperamental, impulsive, and feckless.
I enjoy gasconade
and a foolish tirade.
My unbalance is hopelessly checkless.

Are my nuclear threats just a ruse?
All the pundits are searching for clues.
Since we bought all that stuff,
talk's not nearly enough.
Why have WMDs we won't use?[76]

CHARLOTTESVILLE[77]
AUGUST 13, 2017

White supremacists, Nazis, and Klan
all repeatedly claim I'm their man.
I'll keep "making us great"
by mainstreaming their hate.
Flames of bigotry I love to fan.

I'll continue to falsely conflate
the purveyors and victims of hate.
I would never pick fights
with my dunce acolytes.
Their racism I won't denigrate.

MORE CHARLOTTESVILLE
AUGUST 14, 2017

All those critics are so quick to pounce
on my failure to firmly renounce
the vile acts of my base
and their baiting of race.
Homegrown terror's too hard to pronounce.

I've established white nationalist cred:
on my birther nonsense they're well fed.
I support alt-right creed.
It's their votes that I need.
Flatter me and I'll jump in your bed.

And later in the day:

I was finally forced to condemn
perpetrators of racist mayhem.
I now sadly concede
(with a tight script to read)
that they're not quite the crème de la crème.[78]

CHARLOTTESVILLE REDUX
(IMAGINING TRUMP RECOGNIZES HIS WILD FLIP-FLOPS BUT CAN'T HELP HIMSELF)
AUGUST 15, 2017

Trouble follows my every ad lib—
inarticulate, foolish, not glib.
I spout uninformed drivel.
About "fake news" I'll snivel.
Maybe Kelly should get me a bib.

As unfiltered, unhinged Donald Trump,
I now angrily take to the stump.
Working without a script,
all sane pretense is stripped
as my head returns home to my rump.[79]

MORE REFLECTIONS ON CHARLOTTESVILLE
AUGUST 16, 2017

The Klan rally had many fine folks.
They wear supercool white hoods and cloaks.
These reports that they're bad
make me angry and sad.
It's another news media hoax.

And what's wrong with a Nazi salute?
Only Jews and non-whites give a hoot.
A devoted "Seig Heil"
will bring many a smile,
as my rhetoric starts to bear fruit.

So they chanted about blood and soil,
which caused sensitive liberals to boil.
Don't those touchy Jews know
it was so long ago?
There's no longer a need to recoil.

It's real hard to find where fault resides.
Like a circle it has many sides.
Or would that be a square?
Well, I really don't care.
Race relations are making great strides.

AMERICA: HEEL!
AUGUST 19, 2017

I don't know why it's such a big dele
that I never learned how to spell heal.
It's one miner misteak,
so just give me a brake.
That's not why they put me at the wiel.

It's two hard to express how I feal.
That's no reason to call me a hele.
And I want to be cleer
that my tweets are sin sear.
You can find moor @donaldtrumpreal.

 **Donald J. Trump** ✔
@realDonaldTrump

 ✔ Follow

Our great country has been divided for decades. Sometimes you
need protest in order to heel, & we will heel, & be stronger than
ever before!

4:34 PM - Aug 19, 2017

TOTAL ECLIPSE OF THE BRAIN[80]
AUGUST 21, 2017

To observe an event this terrific,
I employ techniques unscientific.
Since most scientists lie,
their advice I'll defy.
Why's my eyesight becoming horrific?

JOE ARPIAO HATES CINCO DE MAYO[81]
AUGUST 26, 2017

I consider it sweet and beguiling
when a sheriff does racial profiling.
Joe was held in contempt,
but I'll make him exempt
just to keep white supremacists smiling.

DACA[82]
SEPTEMBER 6, 2017

I love dreamers with all of my heart.
Such a shame that they'll have to depart.
It's the fault of Obama.
He created this drama.
I'm just giving these kids a fresh start.

I'm rescinding this program because
it's against our most cherished of laws.
But if Congress won't act,
I'll keep DACA intact.
Does this mean that my reasoning has flaws?

STORMY WEATHER
(OR AN INCONVENIENT AND EXPENSIVE TRUTH)
SEPTEMBER 12, 2017

Harvey victims endured a bad run.
So I told them to go and have fun.[83]
Though they've lost all their stuff,
there's no need to be gruff.
Can't lose more if your assets are none.

For the victims of Irma I care.[84]
After all, I have properties there.
But to pay for this squall,
must I give up my wall?
That would throw my base into despair.

PERSONAL TREASURY[85]
SEPTEMBER 14, 2017

They complain that my cash man Mnuchin
has engaged in some taxpayer moochin'.
But it seems quite okay
that the public should pay
to fund Steve's honeymoon hoochie-coochin'.

PLAYING IN THE SANDBOX
SEPTEMBER 22, 2017

In my speech to the United Nations,
I released many pent-up frustrations:
dissed our deal with Iran,
called a guy "Rocket Man,"
showed my mastery of foreign relations.[86]

I don't find much in life that is sweeter
than provoking a hostile world leader.
There's no grand strategy—
it just satisfies me.
Childish blurts from an impulsive tweeter.

In response, that Korean blowhard
had the nerve to call me a "dotard."
I don't know what he meant,
but as your president,
I'll trade insults with zero holds barred.[87]
(And be hoisted by my own petard.)

KAEPERNICK AND FRIENDS
SEPTEMBER 23, 2017

Nazi slogans don't cause me to twitch.
And Klan rallies are just harmless kitsch.
But go down on one knee,
seeking equality?
Then I think you're a son of a bitch.[88]

"Son of a Bitch."

— The President

"Very fine people."

— The President

RELIEF FOR PUERTO RICO[89]
SEPTEMBER 28, 2017

I consider it so sad and haunting
that the folks in PR are found wanting.
About aid I've no bones,
but some fellow named Jones
makes assistance impossibly daunting.

They all say it's a rule I can waive,
but I'm struggling with why I should save
people far out to sea
with skin browner than me,
in a debt-ridden island enclave.

I've been told they need water and food,
but right now I'm in too bad a mood,
'cause pro athletes won't stand
for the flag of our land,
which I think is incredibly rude.

Now my government's finally trying,
but that Cruz lady claims they're still dying.
This is such a tough gig,
since the ocean is big.
So those ingrates should stop all their crying.

TOO PRICEY
SEPTEMBER 29, 2017

HHS Secretary Tom Price
chartered aircraft without thinking twice.
Did some stuff that's real silly—
flew from D.C. to Philly!
Even I know that doesn't look nice.[90]

My appointees are falling like leaves.
When they go, hardly anyone grieves.
Though their loss I bemoan,
I've established the tone:
from a swamp to a thick den of thieves.

ISLAND PARADISE[91]
OCTOBER 3, 2017

I'm in PR to help celebrate
the fact that our aid efforts are great.
Only sixteen have died,
which just fills me with pride.
And my towel-throwing skills are first-rate.

MORON[92]
OCTOBER 4, 2017

That Rex Tillerson called me a moron,
making certain his days will be bygone.
He's created a mess
with this one lucky guess.
I need sycophants I can rely on.

POLITICAL STUNT MAN[93]
OCTOBER 8, 2017

Pency left the game at my request
just to protest the players' protest.
Might have cost half a mil
on the taxpayers' bill,
but my base is extremely impressed.

SUBSIDIES
(BUT ONLY FOR THE WEALTHY)[94]
OCTOBER 18, 2017

I'll make insurance subsidies stop
To ensure ACA is a flop.
Congress could reinstate,
which I think would be great.
Is this more of my cranial slop?"

My advisors are growing insistent
that the signals I send be consistent.
So I'm changing my mind:
such relief won't be signed.
I'm remaining Obama resistant.

In the meantime I'll seek to relax
the large burdens I suffer in tax.
Life is really a bitch
when you're privileged and rich.
Why keep lifting the poor on our backs?

COMPASSIONATE CONDOLENCES[95]
OCTOBER 23, 2017

I'm the champion of soldiers who've fallen.
To their families I'm writin' and callin'.
I show great sympathy.
No one's better than me!
And Obama's approach was appallin'.

Their kids ended up victims of war
but knew what they were signing up for.
They did not die in vain
or get caught like McCain.[96]
So there's no reason they should be sore.

TRUTH TO POWER[97]
OCTOBER 24, 2017

McCain said my agenda's half-baked,
and today my frail ego got Flaked.
Then there's "liddle" Bob Corker
bringing down this New Yorker,
while McConnell and Ryan still quaked.

INDICTMENT EXCITEMENT[98]
OCTOBER 31, 2017

The indictment of Paul Manafort
torments me like a genital wart.
We were barely acquainted,
yet the press claims I'm tainted.
So I want this whole inquest cut short.

Now that Mueller's arm muscles are flexed,
could it be that Mike Flynn will be next?
As they put on the squeeze,
snitches fall from the trees.
How to tweet this away has me vexed.

Papadopoulos – "Excellent guy!"
Better Clinton dirt, money can't buy.
After copping a plea,
did he tattle on me?
Can't he follow my lead and just lie?

What about Jared, Jeff, little Don?
Pretty soon they will likely be gone.
If I help them make bail,
will the Mueller probe fail?
Would they still reveal I'm the chief con?

It's a plot to prove I'm a bad dude:
that I sought to conspire and collude.
So I'll tweet, rant and pout.
Putin, please help me out!
Without your aid, I'm gonna get screwed!

SUTHERLAND SPRINGS, TEXAS[99]
NOVEMBER 6, 2017

You can shoot forty people with ease,
and I'll call it a mental disease.
But if your repertoire
includes "Allah akbar,"
then it's terror produced overseas.

To all those who were in the crosshairs,
and are dead or confined to wheelchairs,
who were shot through the spleen
with an AR-15:
I am sending sincere thoughts and prayers.

Every week lifeless bodies are strewn,
but I'll keep singing NRA's tune:
While we do sympathize,
let's not "politicize."
For solutions, it's always too soon.

ENDNOTES

1. Trump bitterly complains that the media "lied" when it estimated his inauguration crowd size to be about 250,000. "I made a speech. I looked out. The field was—it looked like a million, a million and a half people." He goes on to state that there were 250,000 right by the stage, and the "rest of the, you know, 20-block area, all the way back to the Washington Monument, was packed." Photos show, however, that the crowd did not extend to the monument, and there were large areas of empty space on the Mall. By contrast, photos of President Obama's 2008 inauguration show a completely packed Mall and a substantially larger crowd. Washington Metro ridership records also support the conclusion that Obama's turnout was much bigger. Nevertheless, White House Press Secretary Sean Spicer announces, in his first media briefing the day after the inauguration, that "[t]his was the largest audience ever to witness an inauguration—period—both in person and around the globe." When asked on NBC's *Meet the Press* why Trump would have his press secretary come to the podium for the first time and utter such a falsehood, White House counselor Kellyanne Conway famously responds that Spicer gave "alternative facts."

2. Iran, Iraq, Libya, Somalia, Sudan, Syria, and Yemen.

3. Trump repeatedly mentions the 9/11 attacks as the reason for this ban. However, none of the 9/11 terrorists were from the countries listed in the ban. Fifteen of the nineteen terrorists were from Saudi Arabia. The rest were from Egypt, the United Arab Emirates, and Lebanon.

4. The Muslim-majority countries in which Trump has business interests are Egypt, Saudi Arabia, Turkey, the United Arab Emirates, Lebanon, and Indonesia.

5. In a speech following his victory in the Nevada caucuses in February, 2016, Trump declares, "We won with the poorly educated. I love the poorly educated." A year later, Trump nominates Betsy DeVos for the position of education secretary. DeVos is a wealthy donor to the Republican Party, who is known for her support of school choice, school voucher programs, and charter schools. All her education was in private schools. She is confirmed in the Senate by a 51–50 vote, with Vice President Pence casting the deciding vote. It is the first time in history that a vice president has had to cast the deciding vote to confirm a cabinet nominee.

6. On February 11, 2017, Trump has lunch with Japanese Prime Minister Shinzo Abe at Trump's Mar-a-Lago resort in Florida. Several cabinet members and close advisors are in attendance. During the lunch meeting, which takes place in a terrace dining room where Mar-a-Lago club members are also present, Trump receives a call on his cell phone advising that North Korea has launched an intermediate-range ballistic missile. The meeting quickly morphs into a strategy discussion.

Club members observe the unfolding events, report them to members of the press, and post pictures of them on social media.

7. On February 13, 2017, General Michael Flynn resigns as Trump's national security advisor. Flynn states, with White House concurrence, that he resigned because he had not been forthcoming with Vice President Mike Pence about interactions with government officials, including a meeting prior to Trump taking office in which Flynn had discussed removing sanctions imposed by the Obama administration because of Russian interference with the presidential election.

8. Weeks prior to Flynn's resignation, Acting Attorney General Sally Yates warned Trump administration officials of Flynn's connection with the Russians. She expressed grave concern that Flynn's situation vis-à-vis the Russians made him vulnerable to blackmail and therefore a danger to national security. The administration delayed taking any action regarding Flynn, however, until news reports surfaced concerning these matters.

9. Alex Jones is a far-right radio show host and the proprietor of *Infowars*, an Internet blog that peddles conspiracy theories such as the notion that the Oklahoma City bombing, the 9/11 terror attacks, and the Sandy Hook school shooting were "false flag" operations perpetrated by the government to gain more power. Jones claims that the child deaths at Sandy Hook were staged and that nobody was hurt. He is an ardent Trump supporter, has spoken at Trump rallies, and has had Trump as a guest on his radio show. Trump, who subscribes to conspiracy theories himself (e.g., birtherism), has praised Jones for his "amazing reputation."

10. No evidence ever has been presented to support the claim that Obama wiretapped Trump Tower.

11. In an extremely awkward moment at the White House in front of television cameras, Trump ignores German chancellor Angela Merkel's offer of a handshake.

12. During the first two months of his presidency, Trump signs a deluge of executive orders, many of them undermining or undoing initiatives of the Obama administration, including trade agreements, environmental protections, educational funding, and Affordable Care Act (Obamacare) funding.

13. The United States attacks Syria's Shayrat airbase with Tomahawk missiles on April 6, 2017. Some planes and infrastructure are destroyed, but the runway is left intact. The next day, Syrian fighter planes are seen taking off from the same base.

14. On March 10, 2017, NBC reporter Katy Tur tweets that it appears Spicer is wearing his flag lapel pin upside down. The next day, she mocks him for complaining about questions from NBC colleagues Hallie Jackson and Peter Alexander: "It's called journalism." Trump has made his disdain for Tur clear on many occasions, including during the campaign when he singled her out twice at rallies as an example of the "dishonest press."

15. For more on Trump's attitude concerning female television journalists, see the verse entitled Bloody Women.

16. At a press conference on April 11, 2017, Spicer claims that, unlike Syrian President Bashar al Assad, Adolf Hitler never stooped to the level of using chemical weapons. He later apologizes for these remarks and acknowledges that Hitler used chemical gas to exterminate millions of Jews.

17. In fact, Spicer later gets caught hiding in the bushes to avoid immediately answering reporter questions about the Comey firing.

18. Saturday Night Live performers, led by Melissa McCarthy, mercilessly mock Spicer on a continuing basis.

19. On May 9, 2017, Trump fires FBI Director James Comey. Comey recently had testified before Congress, confirming that he is actively investigating Russian attempts to influence the presidential election outcome and the potential role of the Trump campaign in that effort. Comey learns that he is fired from television news that is playing in the background while he addresses a meeting of the bureau in Los Angeles.

20. In an interview in *The Economist*, Trump uses the phrase "prime the pump" when asked about his new tax plan's potential to increase the deficit. He then says to the interviewer, "Have you heard that expression before? Because I haven't heard it. I mean, I just…I came up with it a couple of days ago, and I thought it was good." The saying, however, has been around for decades and is commonly used in economics discussions. In fact, it was used by Trump himself in an interview for *Time Magazine* several months earlier.

21. Deputy Attorney General Rod Rosenstein authors a three-page memo that is used by Trump to justify the firing of FBI Director James Comey. Trump later admits in an interview by Lester Holt of NBC News that he already had made up his mind to fire Comey and that it was because of the FBI director's continued pursuit of an investigation into Russian intermeddling in the presidential election.

22. The day after firing Comey, Trump meets behind closed doors in the Oval Office with Russian Foreign Minister Sergei Lavrov and Russian Ambassador Sergey Kislyak. No American reporters or photographers are allowed in the room, but a photographer for the Russia state-run newspaper *TASS* is present. The next day, photographs from the meeting are widely circulated. Administration officials express surprise and claim that the Russian press has tricked them by releasing the photographs.

23. The so-called Emoluments Clause (Article 1, Section 8) of the U.S. Constitution states that no holder of public office may, without consent of Congress, "accept any present, emolument, office, or title of any kind whatever, from any King, Prince, or Foreign State." The purpose of the clause is to prevent conflicts of interest. In late January, 2017, a watchdog organization called Citizens for Responsibility and Ethics in Washington filed a lawsuit against Trump, alleging that he is violating this clause by permitting payments to his businesses by foreign governments. Since that time, three additional lawsuits of a similar nature have been filed against Trump. As of the date of this publication, all those suits are still pending.

24. During his meeting with Russian officials Lavrov and Kislyak, Trump reveals highly classified information about the Islamic State. In doing so, he potentially jeopardizes the source of the information, which turns out to be Israel.

25. A few days after the reports that Trump has disclosed classified information to the Russians, his National Security Advisor H. R. McMaster holds a press briefing in which he haltingly and halfheartedly tries to defend Trump's actions, an awkward moment for the decorated general.

26. On May 17, 2017, Deputy Attorney General Rod Rosenstein announces his appointment of Robert Mueller to serve as special counsel in the investigation of Russian interference with the presidential election and the Trump campaign's potential role in that endeavor.

27. At the NATO meeting in Brussels, Belgium, Trump shoves Montenegro's prime minister out of the way so he can position himself in front during a photo shoot, castigates NATO members for failing to keep up in their payments, and states (contradicting his own campaign assertions) that NATO "is no longer obsolete."

28. During a closed-door EU meeting in Brussels, Trump decries Germany's trade surplus with the United States, saying, "Look at the millions of cars they sell in the USA. Terrible. We will stop that."

29. On May 25, 2017, the U.S. Court of Appeals for the Fourth Circuit upholds a lower court order enjoining indefinitely the Trump administration's revised travel ban.

30. *New York Magazine* discovers and reports a $2 trillion calculation error in the 2018 budget announced by Trump's treasury secretary, Steve Mnuchin, due to the fact that the same number has been counted twice. Former Treasury Secretary Larry Summers states that such a miscalculation would justify a failing grade for a math student. Discovery of the error negates Trump administration claims that its proposed tax cut for the rich would "pay for itself."

31. On June 1, 2017, Trump announces the withdrawal of the United States from the Paris Climate Agreement, to which 195 nations are signatory. The agreement is designed to achieve global cooperation in protecting the environment. Trump justifies his action on the basis that it imposes "unfair" restrictions on American businesses and workers.

32. On June 16, 2017, after hinting for weeks that he would do so, Trump announces new restrictions on travel and commercial relationships between the United States and Cuba, rolling back some of the rapprochement initiated during the Obama administration. As a rationale, Trump cites the Cuban government's repression of its citizens and its lack of democratic elections, a seemingly hypocritical stance in view of his desire for closer ties with other repressive totalitarian regimes.

33. A memo written by James Comey after an Oval Office meeting with Trump in February reveals that Trump had told him, "I hope you can let this go," referring to his investigation of then National Security Advisor Michael Flynn's Russia connection.

34. Members of Congress, reporters, and pundits debate whether Trump's expression of "hope" to Comey is a threat, an order, or simply a harmless aspirational statement.

35. After Comey's testimony before Congress, Trump claims that Comey lied about his request to spare Flynn. He also disputes Comey's assertion that he had asked for Comey's loyalty. When a reporter asks Trump if he would be willing to testify under oath before Congress, Trump responds, "One hundred percent." Marc Kasowitz is serving as Trump's outside legal counsel at this time.

36. Following Comey's testimony, Trump asserts that "James Comey better hope that there are no 'tapes' of our conversations…" For the next forty-one days, Trump hedges in response to questions from the press as to whether there are White House tape recordings before finally admitting that none exist. In the meantime, because of Trump's refusal to clarify his statement and

indicate whether recordings were made, the House Intelligence Committee issues a subpoena for such recordings.

37. On June 12, 2017, Trump holds his first full cabinet meeting inside the White House. He begins the meeting by extolling the many alleged accomplishments of his administration and then asks the cabinet members to introduce themselves. One by one, in front of television cameras, they heap praise on Trump and thank him for the opportunity to serve in his administration.

38. Also on June 12, 2017, Trump surrogates tell the press that he is considering firing Special Counsel Robert Mueller. After immediate denunciation of such a move by members of Congress on both sides of the aisle, Trump spokesperson Sarah Huckabee Sanders denies any intention to terminate Mueller. However, the White House effort to discredit Mueller's investigation as a witch hunt continues.

39. Trump reportedly is "furious" with Attorney General Jeff Sessions over his recusal from the investigation into Russia's intermeddling with the election. In a press briefing on June 7, less than a week before Sessions's scheduled testimony before the Senate Intelligence Committee, Press Secretary Sean Spicer refuses to say whether Trump still has confidence in Sessions.

40. James Comey, Sally Yates (former acting attorney general, who tried to warn the Trump administration about Michael Flynn's Russia ties and his vulnerability to blackmail), and Preet Bharara (former U.S. Attorney for the Southern District of New York, who was directing a criminal investigation into Trump's business dealings) all have been fired by Trump.

41. In its decision striking down the Trump administration's revised travel ban, the U.S. Court of Appeals for the Ninth Circuit cites Trump's own statements to decipher intent, including his tweets.

42. Dennis Rodman, former NBA player and contestant on *The Apprentice*, goes to North Korea. Rodman reportedly has a good relationship with North Korean leader Kim Jong-Un. Rodman declines to say whether he is there at the Trump administration's behest. A day after Rodman's arrival, a U.S. citizen who has been held prisoner in North Korea for seventeen months is released. The Trump administration denies that there is any connection between Rodman's visit and the prisoner's release.

43. On June 13, 2017, Jeff Sessions testifies before the Senate Intelligence Committee. He repeatedly refuses to answer questions about his discussions with Trump concerning the Russia investigation and the Comey firing, citing executive privilege. Several senators point out that the

President has not asserted that privilege as a bar to Sessions's testimony on the subject. Sessions responds that the privilege potentially could be asserted by Trump. The senators dispute that such a "potential" provides a legal basis for refusing to answer questions.

44. During his testimony, Sessions is clearly flustered by the aggressive and skillful questioning of California Senator (and former California Attorney General) Kamala Harris. Here, as in previous hearings, Harris is repeatedly cut off by male senators on the other side of the aisle.

45. A van plows into Muslim worshippers outside a mosque in London. In contrast to his approach when Muslims are the perpetrators, Trump has nothing to say.

46. During the Republican presidential candidate debates, moderator Megyn Kelly of Fox News asks Trump a question about his misogynistic statements. Afterward, in an interview with CNN's Jake Tapper, Trump predictably calls her "overrated." He also says, "You could see there was blood coming out of her eyes. Blood coming out of her wherever."

47. Trump's proposed budget reduces funding for Medicaid by approximately $800 million, contrary to his campaign promise not to make cuts to that program. The budget also takes into account anticipated tax cuts for the wealthy.

48. When the New Jersey legislature fails to reach a budget compromise by the Fourth of July weekend, nonessential services are closed, including Island Beach State Park, which is just outside Governor Chris Christie's state-owned residence. Governor Christie, whose popularity (15 percent) is even lower than Trump's, takes his family to the closed beach for some fun in the sun. Unbeknown to the Christies, their excursion is being photographed by a drone. When later confronted with the evidence by reporters, Christie responds, "That's just the way it goes. Run for governor, and you can have a residence."

49. At the G-20 meeting on July 7, 2007, Trump criticizes the competence of U.S. intelligence agencies, saying they got it wrong about weapons of mass destruction in Iraq and questioning their conclusion about Russian meddling in the 2016 presidential election.

50. On July 8, 2017, the *New York Times* runs a story about Donald Trump Jr. having met with a Russian lawyer along with other Trump campaign officials prior to the election. Junior's first response to the story is to characterize the meeting as one about adoption. He fails to mention anything about an offer by the Russian attorney to provide dirt on Hillary Clinton. Only when it becomes apparent that the *Times* is about to publish a much more detailed account of the meeting does Junior admit it was set up for the purpose of obtaining Clinton information.

51. Upon greeting Mrs. Macron, Trump says, "You're in good shape. She's in such good physical shape. Beautiful."

52. Trump issues an official proclamation designating July 16–22, 2017 as "Made in America Week," to celebrate and promote U.S. manufacturing.

53. Almost all of Ivanka Trump's clothing line is manufactured overseas: China, India, Indonesia, Bangladesh, and Vietnam.

54. Three Republican senators (Murkowski of Alaska, Capito of West Virginia, and Collins of Maine) say they will oppose a procedural vote to advance Senate Majority Leader Mitch McConnell's plan to repeal significant portions of Obamacare without a replacement plan in place. The repeal effort seems dead, but McConnell says he isn't giving up. Trump is angry. He offers no solutions but wants Congress to forego the August recess until they can get it done.

55. On July 19, 2017, Trump gives a rambling, accusatory, self-aggrandizing, inarticulate, and often incoherent interview to the *New York Times*. Words do not suffice to describe it. A transcript is available on the Internet.

56. As Trump grows more impatient and concerned about the ongoing special counsel investigation and its apparent expansion into his personal business dealings, including potential money-laundering schemes with Russian oligarchs, he reportedly asks his attorneys about his options, including whether he can pardon colleagues, family members, and even himself.

57. At the annual National Scout Jamboree on July 24, 2017, Trump gives a highly political speech to forty thousand boy scouts, in which he boasts about his "record" crowd size, criticizes "fake media," and bashes both Barack Obama and Hillary Clinton. He also threatens to fire his health and human services secretary if Obamacare repeal doesn't pass in Congress. Over the past eighty years, all previous presidents who have spoken at this event stayed away from partisan politics and instead addressed such topics as good citizenship. Members of both parties and the press react negatively to Trump's speech.

58. While campaigning in Iowa in July, 2015, Trump famously said about Arizona Senator John McCain, "He's not a war hero. He's a war hero only because he was captured. I like people who weren't captured."

59. In one last-ditch effort to pass some kind of legislation regarding Obamacare, McConnell pushes "skinny repeal," in which fewer sections of the law are scrapped but still no replacement is

offered. In a dramatic Senate roll call vote in the early morning hours on July 28, 2017, the measure fails 51–49, with Republican Senators Collins, Murkowski, and McCain voting no.

60. On July 26, 2017, Trump tweets that he has decided to ban transgender individuals from serving in any capacity in the U.S. military service. Although his tweets state that he has reached this decision after consultation with his generals and military experts, the military establishment appears to be caught off guard. Among other concerns, Trump's directive contains no guidance about what to do with transgender people currently serving.

61. On July 21, 2017, Trump makes a surprise announcement that blunt-talking Wall Street financier Anthony Scaramucci will become White House communications director. Beleaguered Press Secretary Spicer resigns in protest.

62. Trump, still angry over Sessions's voluntary recusal from the Russian interference investigation, refuses to express confidence in his attorney general or to state that his job is secure. Republican leadership, supporting Sessions, tells Trump that if he fires Sessions, they will not confirm a replacement.

63. On July 28, 2017, Trump fires Chief of Staff Reince Priebus and replaces him with General John Kelly, formerly director of Homeland Security.

64. Conservative columnist Peggy Noonan writes in the *Wall Street Journal* that Trump is "weak and sniveling" and "undermines himself almost daily by ignoring" traditional norms of masculinity. She also says, "He's a drama queen," who engages in "whimpering accusation and finger-pointing" and whose tweets show "utter weakness"

65. On July 26, 2017, Trump's newly appointed White House Communications Director Anthony Scaramucci telephones Ryan Lizza of *New Yorker* magazine and engages in a vulgar rant that Scaramucci mistakenly assumes is off the record. Among other things, Scaramucci declares, "I'm not Steve Bannon. I'm not trying to suck my own cock." Shortly thereafter, it is reported that Scaramucci's wife has decided she's leaving him.

66. On July 31, 2017, apparently on advice of new Chief of Staff Kelly, Trump fires Scaramucci.

67. On July 31, 2017, the *Washington Post* reports that Trump had instructed his son Donald Jr. to tell the press his meeting during the campaign with a Russian lawyer was focused primarily on U.S. adoption of Russian children. E-mails showed that, in fact, the meeting was set up to discuss potentially damaging information the Russians claimed to have about Hillary Clinton. The day

after the *Washington Post* article, White House spokesperson Sarah Huckabee Sanders says Trump only "weighed in, offering suggestions, as any father would do."

68. On August 2, 2017, Trump unveils proposed legislation called the RAISE Act, which would reduce legal immigration by 50 percent over the next ten years and prioritize those who speak English and are well educated.

69. Under Trump, the State Department budget is substantially reduced, many senior positions remain unfilled, and career foreign-service officers are routinely excluded from the decision-making process. Trump exhibits a dismissive attitude toward diplomacy and the diplomats who execute it. Trump's son-in-law, Jared Kushner, who has no diplomatic experience, has become an envoy to foreign leaders, sometimes in place of the Secretary of State Rex Tillerson.

70. On July 31, 2017, General John Kelly is sworn in as the new chief of staff. Trump's daughter Ivanka attends the swearing-in ceremony and tweets, "Looking forward to serving alongside John Kelly as we work for the American people." Ivanka has no official position within the administration, no government experience or credentials, and obviously no understanding of chain of command. On the other hand, Trump runs his administration like a family business.

71. On August 2, 2017, Trump reluctantly signs legislation limiting his authority to lift sanctions imposed on Russia. He calls the legislation flawed and unconstitutional and, in a tweet, blames Congress for poor relations with Russia.

72. Trump tells the *Wall Street Journal* in an interview that he "got a call from the head of the Boy Scouts," saying his address at last month's National Scout Jamboree was "the greatest speech that was ever made to them." He also claims, at a cabinet meeting, that Mexican president Pena Nieto recently had called him and said very few people are coming across Mexico's southern border "because they know they're not going to get to our [U.S.] border, which is the ultimate compliment." The Boy Scouts and Mexican Foreign Ministry, respectively, deny that these calls ever occurred. At a press briefing on August 2, 2017, White House Press Secretary Sanders admits the calls did not happen.

73. "That White House is a real dump," Trump reportedly states to several other golf members before teeing off at Trump National Golf Course in Bedminster, New Jersey, on his first visit there after assuming the presidency. This revelation appears in a *Sports Illustrated* article authored by Alan Shipnuck. The author had confirmed the accuracy of the quote with several individuals who were present at the time. Nonetheless, Trump denies having made the comment.

74. On August 8, 2017, following the revelation that North Korea successfully has miniaturized a nuclear warhead to fit on an intercontinental ballistic missile, Trump holds a televised press conference at his Bedminster, New Jersey, golf resort. He says, with arms folded, "North Korea best not make any more threats to the United States. They will be met with fire, fury and, frankly, power, the likes of which the world has never seen before."

75. On August 9, 2017, the North Korean state-run news agency responds to Trump's threat by saying that its military is "examining the operational plan" to fire medium- and long-range ballistic missiles at the U.S. territory of Guam, including Anderson Air Force Base, to "send a serious warning signal."

76. During the presidential campaign, Trump reportedly asks a foreign-policy expert, on three separate occasions, why we couldn't use nuclear weapons if we have them.

77. Over the weekend of August 12 and 13, 2017, neo-Nazis and white supremacists hold a rally in Charlottesville, Virginia. They wear swastikas and other Nazi insignia, carry torches, chant the Nazi slogan "blood and soil," and use racist and anti-Semitic rhetoric. One of them intentionally drives his car into a crowd of counter-demonstrators, killing a young woman and injuring many others. On August 13, Trump reads from a script denouncing the violence but then departs from his written remarks and blames "many sides." He fails to call out the Ku Klux Klan and neo-Nazis by name. Members of both political parties quickly criticize Trump's stance.

78. On August 14, 2017, in response to the growing criticism of his earlier statement, Trump stands before the cameras and woodenly reads from a script, this time without deviation, specifically decrying the actions of white nationalist organizations.

79. On August 15, 2017, at a press conference and unburdened by any script, Trump defends his initial remarks and reverts to his position that "both sides" were at fault. He says that there were "fine people" participating in the white nationalist rally. Ku Klux Klan leader David Duke, who had attended the rally, tweets a thank-you to Trump for his remarks. Duke had endorsed Trump during the campaign.

80. While normal people use protective eyewear to view the solar eclipse, Trump stares right into it.

81. After hinting he would do so at a rally of supporters, Trump officially pardons former Phoenix, Arizona, Sheriff Joe Arpaio, who had been convicted in federal court of contempt for refusing to abide by an order to cease racial profiling against Latinos.

82. Professing his great affection for the young undocumented individuals protected from deportation under President Obama's Deferred Action for Childhood Arrivals (DACA) program, Trump announces (through Attorney General Sessions) that the program will be rescinded in six months unless Congress acts to keep it in place. He claims that DACA is unconstitutional because a president lacks independent authority to implement it. He then undermines this rationale by hinting that if Congress doesn't take such action, he might reinstate DACA himself.

83. On September 2, 2017, at the conclusion of a visit to a shelter for Hurricane Harvey survivors near Houston, Texas, Trump tells the assembled victims, "Have a good time." The huge hurricane had devastated vast areas of Texas, killing forty-three people and leaving thousands of others homeless and destitute.

84. A few days after Hurricane Harvey ravages Texas and parts of Louisiana, Hurricane Irma rolls through the Caribbean Islands and Florida, causing heavy damage and casualties.

85. On September 13, 2017, Treasury Secretary Steve Mnuchin's office confirms that he had requested use of a U.S. Airforce jet for his honeymoon the previous month to Scotland, France, and Italy. The cost of the jet to taxpayers would have been approximately $25,000 per hour. Mnuchin attempted to justify the request based on the need for "secure communications" during his trip. Typically, the only cabinet members requiring use of government planes are the secretaries of state and defense. Mnuchin later withdrew this request. The disclosure of this request is made as Mnuchin is under investigation by the Treasury Department's inspector general for his use of a military plane for a visit to Kentucky in August, with his new wife, during which they viewed the solar eclipse. Mnuchin is a partner at Goldman Sachs with a net worth of around $300 million.

86. On September 19, 2017, Trump addresses the United Nations General Assembly. During his speech, he threatens to "totally destroy" North Korea and refers to its leader, Kim Jong-Un, as "Rocket Man." He also strongly criticizes the nuclear-arms agreement struck by the Obama administration with Iran.

87. Three days after Trump's United Nations speech, Kim Jong-Un responds by calling him "deranged" and a "dotard," meaning he's aged and becoming senile. Later that day, Trump tweets that Kim is a "madman who doesn't mind starving and killing his own people..." For proper rhyming, in this limerick "dotard" must be given a French pronunciation, with emphasis on the second syllable.

88. Continuing what was started last season by San Francisco 49er Colin Kaepernick, some NFL players go to one knee while the national anthem is played, in protest against police brutality and

other unfair and unequal treatment of African Americans. During a campaign rally for Senator Luther Strange in Alabama on September 22, 2017, Trump decries these protests and states, "Wouldn't you like to see one of those NFL owners, when somebody disrespects the flag, say, 'Get that son of a bitch off the field right now; fire him'?" In the firestorm that ensues from Trump's remarks, entire NFL teams show solidarity with their African American players by locking arms, going to one knee together, or remaining in the locker room during the anthem.

89. The Trump administration is slow to respond to the devastation caused by Hurricane Maria in Puerto Rico. In contrast to its prompt actions assisting Texas, Louisiana, and Florida after Hurricanes Harvey and Irma, the administration waits several days to waive the provisions of the Jones Act, a 1920 federal statute that prevents foreign ships from delivering goods between U.S. ports. As Puerto Rico is a U.S. territory, this makes aid delivery slower and more expensive. When Trump finally does waive the Jones Act restrictions, he makes the waiver temporary (lasting only ten days). Also, rather than personally addressing the unfolding tragedy, he continually tweets about the NFL player protests. When he finally makes public statements about the situation in Puerto Rico, he sounds ambivalent, referring to its heavy debt and its poor infrastructure. Ultimately, the aid effort begins but is criticized as wholly inadequate by Puerto Rican officials, including San Juan Mayor Carmen Yulin Cruz, who gives an emotional statement to the press about the fact that people continue to die from lack of food, water, and basic services due to federal government "inefficiency" and "bureaucracy." In response, Trump lashes out on Twitter at Cruz, accusing her of "poor leadership." He also tweets that the people of Puerto Rico "want everything to be done for them, when it should be a community effort." And while claiming that his administration is doing a "fantastic job," Trump explains that it is difficult to provide aid to Puerto Rico because "[t]his is an island surrounded by water. Big water. Ocean water."

90. On September 29, 2017, Health and Human Services Secretary Tom Price, a so-called budget hawk who had railed against excessive government spending, resigns following a furor over reports that he has been chartering private jets for trips between major hubs, which easily could have been accomplished using far less expensive commercial carriers. Under some estimates, these unnecessary charters cost the taxpayers more than $400,000. Trump comments that while Price is a "very fine man," he is unhappy with the "optics" of Price's actions.

91. On October 3, 2017, Trump visits Puerto Rico. In unscripted remarks, he states how wonderful the weather is, praises his administration's relief efforts, wisecracks about how those efforts are "busting the budget," says that Hurricane Katrina resulted in a much higher death toll, and asserts that Puerto Ricans should be "proud" that their death toll is only sixteen. (In fact, as of that date it had risen to thirty-four.) He also makes a show of tossing paper towels and other supplies to those in attendance.

92. NBC News and other outlets reveal that, during a meeting at the Pentagon in the summer (at which Trump was not present), Secretary of State Rex Tillerson referred to him as a "fucking moron." The reports also state that Tillerson had been on the verge of quitting, but Vice President Pence convinced him to stay. Responding to these stories, Tillerson says that he never considered leaving his post, but does not deny having made the "moron" comment. Trump is reportedly outraged by this revelation.

93. On October 8, 2017, Vice President Mike Pence attends an NFL game in Indianapolis between the Colts and the San Francisco 49ers. As expected, since they had been doing it for several games, a number of 49ers players kneel during the national anthem to protest racial injustice. Pence, having warned reporters ahead of time that he might not be around long, abruptly leaves the game after the anthem. Shortly afterward, he tweets that he left because he found the kneeling disrespectful to the flag, the country, and its veterans. Not to be out-tweeted, Trump chimes in that he had asked Pence to leave the game if any of the players kneeled during the anthem and that he is proud of Pence for doing so. News media appropriately label Pence's appearance, his abrupt departure, and the subsequent tweets as an orchestrated political stunt. They point out that for this public relations show, Pence's air travel costs alone would approach a quarter million dollars and that significantly more was spent on Secret Service presence and advance security work, to be paid with tax dollars.

94. On October 14, 2017, Trump signs an executive order eliminating the "cost-sharing" subsidies paid under Obamacare to insurers for providing less expensive plans for low-income Americans. Trump's former chief strategist Steve Bannon praises Trump for taking this action, stating that it is "gonna blow that thing [Obamacare] up." Trump later tells reporters, "Obamacare is finished. It's dead. It's gone. You shouldn't even mention it. It's gone. There's no such thing as Obamacare anymore." Then, after learning of a bipartisan plan among senators to maintain the subsidies for a two-year period (thereby avoiding the loss of health insurance by millions of Americans) while improvements to Obamacare are negotiated, Trump implies that he would sign such legislation. He states that it is "a short-term solution so that we don't have this very dangerous little period… and it will get us over this immediate hump." However, White House spokespersons thereafter indicate that Trump would not sign this legislation if it came to his desk. Meanwhile, Trump continues to tout his "tax reform" plan, which would substantially reduce federal income taxes for the wealthiest one percent while presenting little or no tax relief for low and middle income Americans.

95. During a press briefing on October 16, 2017, Trump deflects questions about his failure for twelve days to make any comment concerning the death of four Marines during an ISIS ambush in Niger. Instead, he claims that unlike his predecessors in office, and specifically President

Obama, he both writes and makes phone calls to the families of soldiers killed in action. This provokes a storm of factual repudiations and criticisms. In addition, presumably as a result of Trump's assertion, Representative Frederica Wilson of Florida tells the press that she was present and listening on the speakerphone when Trump called the pregnant widow of a soldier from her district (one of the four killed in Niger) and told her, "Well, I guess he knew what he signed up for." The congresswoman, a friend of the soldier and his family, was traveling in a car with the widow on the way to the airport to meet her husband's casket when Trump called. Trump angrily denies having made any such statement to the widow, calling it "totally fabricated," and claims to have proof of this. However, the congresswoman's story is corroborated by the soldier's aunt, who also was present during the telephone call. Chief of Staff John Kelly, while attempting to defend Trump in a press briefing, also appears to corroborate this version of events, saying that those words are similar to ones used (albeit more artfully) by a military officer who tried to comfort him after his son was killed in battle. General Kelly tells reporters that he had advised Trump not to call the families of these fallen soldiers but when Trump rejected this advice and asked what he should say, Kelly recounted the substance of condolences offered to him. On October 23, in an ABC News interview, the soldier's widow confirms the congresswoman's version. Trump never presents his "proof" to the contrary.

96. See note 58.

97. Trump finally begins to hear harsh criticism from within his own party. Senator John McCain, in a speech in Philadelphia on October 16, 2017, refers to the administration's isolationist policies as "half- baked spurious nationalism, cooked up by people who would rather find scapegoats than solve problems." Senator Jeff Flake, in a speech to fellow legislators on October 24, 2017, specifically calls out Trump for "the personal attacks, the threats against principles, freedoms, and institutions, the flagrant disregard for truth and decency, the reckless provocations, most often for the pettiest and most personal reasons; reasons having nothing whatsoever to do with the fortunes of the people that we have all been elected to serve." The same day, in an interview with news reporters, Senator Bob Corker says that "[t]he debasement of our nation will be what [Trump is] remembered most for…" In typical fashion, Trump responds with personally insulting statements about Corker and Flake. In previous tweets, Trump had referred to Corker as "liddle" Bob, who "couldn't get elected dog catcher." Meanwhile, other members of Republican Party leadership, most notably Mitch McConnell and Paul Ryan, remain silent about Trump's transgressions and refuse to comment on these developments, stating that they wish instead to remain focused on the party's agenda.

98. On October 30, 2017, the office of special counsel Robert Mueller announces the filing of criminal charges against three former Trump campaign aides: Paul Manafort, Richard Gates, and

George Papadopoulos. Manafort had been Trump's campaign manager for several months and Gates had served as Manafort's top deputy. Papadopoulos was one of Trump's foreign policy advisors during the campaign. When announcing the appointment of Papadopoulos in March, 2016, Trump had referred to him as "an excellent guy." The indictments against Manafort and Gates charge them with several counts of fraud, conspiracy and money laundering during a time frame starting before and continuing through their association with the Trump campaign. It also is disclosed that Papadopoulos, charged earlier with lying to the FBI concerning his contacts with Russian agents to obtain "dirt" on Hillary Clinton for the Trump campaign, had pleaded guilty in early October, 2017, and had become a cooperative witness in Mueller's investigation. Legal analysts speculate that the charges will be used to leverage receipt of more information about possible collusion with Russia by the Trump team. In response to this news, the White House attempts to distance itself from the named aides and their alleged actions. Sources reveal, however, that Trump is enraged by the indictments and extremely concerned about the potential consequences.

99. On November 5, 2017, a gunman enters a church in rural Texas and shoots congregants with a Ruger AR Assault-type rifle, killing twenty-six and injuring another twenty. The victims range in age from eighteen months to seventy-seven years. Some of the victims, including children, are shot repeatedly at point-blank range. It is just one of the many mass shootings occurring within the United States in recent years, and takes place only one month after a Las Vegas massacre in which a gunman firing a semi-automatic weapon from a hotel window killed fifty-eight and wounded hundreds. The day after the Texas incident, Trump is asked whether he now will seek any type of gun control legislation, specifically better "vetting" of those who seek to purchase them. Trump responds that it is "too soon" to have such a discussion, and goes on to label the incident a "mental health problem at the highest level," as opposed to a "guns situation." This response echoes the NRA's longstanding position in the aftermath of mass shootings. It directly contrasts with Trump's immediate and vehement response to the ISIS-inspired murder of several bicyclists in New York City a week earlier by a native of Uzbekistan who had lived in the United States for seven years. In that case, Trump had called for more "extreme vetting" of immigrants as an antidote. Adding to the hypocrisy of Trump's reaction to the Texas shooting is the fact that in February, 2017, he signed legislation revoking an Obama administration regulation aimed at making it more difficult for people with a history of mental illness to purchase guns.

SKETCHBOOK

Here are some also-rans that didn't make the cut, but still deserved a home. Enjoy the B-sides!

- Chris

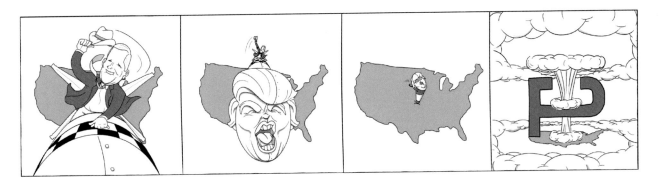

ABOUT THE AUTHOR

Bob Stone is a retired attorney living in Los Angeles, California. Other than the practice of law, his only skills are lifeguarding and writing limericks. Since his aging body is no longer compatible with saving lives (and wearing a speedo would be inappropriate), he has concluded that it is more sensible to spend his spare time composing doggerel. He hopes that despite the efforts of the current administration, his children and grandchildren will be able to live in a safer, healthier, and more tolerant world.

Photo by Lee Whittam

ABOUT THE ILLUSTRATOR

Chris Critelli is an actor/singer/writer/doodler living in Brooklyn, New York.

www.chriscritelli.com

Photo by Aaron Phillips

Made in the USA
Middletown, DE
12 December 2017